Dazzling
SCARS

Dazzling SCARS

A Self-Help Book

Audrey G. Adams

Divine Purpose Book Publishing
Valdosta, Georgia

Dazzling **SCARS**

Published by
Divine Purpose Book Publishing
Valdosta, Georgia
audrey.adams528@gmail.com

Audrey G. Adams, Publisher / Editorial Director
Yvonne Rose/Quality Press.info, Book Packager

Copyright © 2024 by Audrey G. Adams
ISBN #: 979-8-8693-1741-4
Library of Congress Control Number: 2024907973

Dedication

I would like to dedicate this book to my three Guardian Angels in Heaven. First and foremost, to my Daughter, Jasmine Whitfield, who passed away on January 20, 2000, as well as, my Brother, Gregory Adams, who was a year older than me and passed away on March 8, 2003, of a brain aneurysm.

Also, in dedication to the first man I ever loved, my Dad, Roger D. Adams, who passed away on October 8, 2021. He always encouraged me with many inspiring words and advice. During our conversations about future success, he always advised me to recognize my talents so I would always have a career to fall back on. The times he may have thought I was not listening were the times I absorbed it all. I appreciate all he instilled in me; the advice that stood out the most was, "If you do what you love, you will never work a day in your life." *So, here I am.*

Acknowledgements

I want to give special thanks to God, my personal Savior, for giving me the passion to write. Most importantly, I thank Him for walking alongside me through every step I have taken during my life journey.

To my Mom, Mary Adams, who is the strong woman who gave me life and has been my biggest supporter, no matter what. To my sisters, Yolanda Adams and Agnes Rowland, thank you for always being on my side through some of the hardest times of my life.

A special thank you to my daughter, Kamiila Smith, for being my right hand, my best friend. Thank you for experiencing all aspects of life with me and for never judging me despite my decisions and mistakes.

To my Granddaughter, Lyrik McCloud, you have been a joyous blessing in Mimi's life.

To a few of my close friends who have supported me, thank you all. You know who you are.

I give much gratitude to my Coach, Hario Ovadtop, and the Huddle for being such a huge inspiration during a life-changing moment in my life. I'm truly grateful for each and every one of you. I cannot thank you all enough. I am forever grateful that we crossed paths.

Preface

This self-help book will address some common issues that some of us may have encountered related to self-love and relationships developed with others through dating. Therefore, this book will explain what made me snap back into reality of how I was experiencing the same results in different relationships. So, for everyone who asks themselves, "Why do I keep getting into the same relationships where people use me and abuse me?" and "Why has every relationship I have been involved in led me nowhere?" this book is for you.

First and foremost, you are not alone. The disappointments and the pain you have endured do not define who you are. The only difference between you and others is that some of us use our voice and some choose to remain silent. Through recognition and growth, those wounds become dazzling scars that create a strong and wise soul.

At the end of each chapter, there will be some questions that you can answer in regard to your relationship history with yourself and through your relationships with others. To an advantage, answering these self-evaluation questions will help you determine what weaknesses you have and what steps you can take to help you achieve better results through growth. I will discuss this a little more in another chapter later in this book.

Contents

Introduction

Hello ladies and gentlemen. Let me begin by introducing myself. My name is Audrey. I am a 41-year-old woman, Daughter, Mother, and Grandmother, who has been through many different walks of life. These walks of life include pain, joy, grief, and healing. My journey has inspired me to share information with you that may encourage you or someone you may know concerning the relationship you have with yourself or with others.

The first step of this self-help book is acknowledging that there is a scar within you that contributes to the formation of unhealthy relationships. Do not be ashamed. You are not the first, nor the last human being to go through the common obstacles of life. We all have scars, and those scars have either kept us in our comfort zones or they have driven us to change.

A scar signifies pain endured. Whether pain or joy, what we experience in life will always leave a mark. We get to determine how we will use that scar. Will we hold onto it as a crutch that keeps us in a constant state of wrongdoing, or will we use it as an opportunity to become better? The trials, hardships, and battlefields we have endured only symbolize what we have either fought through or what we have been constantly careless about. The change you crave begins where the problem resides, and that is within YOU!

Chapter 1

The Hard Truth

Welcome, my people, to the hard truth. This chapter is where I am blunt and raw about what you "need" to hear versus what you "want" to hear. Sugarcoating a situation will only hurt us more than the cold-blooded truth. Regardless of the type of situation you are struggling with, within yourself, or in your relationships with others, there are always areas for improvement. Analysis of self is the step that will help you recognize what it is that continues to attract certain types of characteristics in people who always end up hurting you. You have to ask yourself, "Is it really them who keeps hurting me," or "Is it me hurting myself?"

We have to look deep inside ourselves and ask, "Why do I continue to experience the same scenarios?" At some point in your life, you have to realize that no circumstance will change until you can be bold and true to yourself about what part of your being continues to attract these dead-end relationships. Remember, the hard truth will be the first step in making the necessary changes in your life.

On the next page, there are a couple of questions that you can answer to help assist in your personal growth.

Self-Evaluation Questions

1. Do I consider myself to have boundaries?

____

____

2. Do I offer more to others than I receive in return?

____

____

3. What can I do differently that will allow me to focus more on myself than on pleasing others?

____

____

4. Do I recognize the underlying problem?

____

____

Chapter 2

"Why Me?"

"Why Me?" is a common question we often ask ourselves when life does not go the way we anticipate. First and foremost, we have to eliminate the pity party that we create out of pain in order to gain sympathy and attention from others. As for myself, I had to acknowledge that aside from my Savior, the Lord Jesus Christ, I am the main decision-maker that is set forth in my life. Taking accountability for what nonsense we have allowed to occupy our time and life will help us to become more cautious as to what we choose to use our energy on in the future.

Being able to come to terms with what you have allowed and why will give you a better insight into how you can do things differently and not receive the same results. For example, if someone asks you if you can do a monetary favor or something you know will create an unfortunate circumstance for you, but you choose to do it anyway to please them, you have to know that it probably will not result in something positive.

Have you ever been in the presence of an individual or a group of people and you don't feel right? Well, this is your spirit, or some may call it their intuition, telling you something is not right about that environment or person. From the word of the wise, "Always take heed to what your intuition is trying to tell you." Despite your age, you are always learning something new. Personally, during the obstacles that I have faced, I asked, "Why Me?" for many years, especially when I had to bury my child when she was three and a half months old. Over time and with the relationship I built with God I began to understand that He makes NO mistakes. Asking ourselves, "Why Me?" only gives us more of a reason to feel sorry for ourselves, and that only results in excuses of why we "think" we cannot achieve a goal or why we don't deserve a truly loving relationship. When we take every disappointment and heartbreak and look at the positive aspect of the situation, is where an opportunity lies. That opportunity is GROWTH.

From my experience, I noticed when I began replacing, "Why Me?" with "What is God Trying to Teach Me?" is when things in my life began to shift. Using the hard truth about yourself and what issue resides within you, along with asking what God is trying to teach you can turn your whole life around. Take this, for example, when you are in school studying lesson one, you cannot move on to lesson two until you pass the test at the end of that first lesson. With that being said, we will continue to repeat the same mishaps and cycles in life until we have learned the lesson behind it.

Now it is your time to decide what changes you can make that will benefit you in your life. *Answer your self-evaluation questions on the next page.*

Self-Evaluation Questions

1. What have I learned about myself through my
    personal obstacles?

    ____

    ____

2. Do I recognize what I could have done differently
    in my relationships?

    ____

    ____

3. Do I consider myself an "easy-going" person with
    an open mind or a stubborn individual who seems to
    learn lessons the hard way?

    ____

    ____

Chapter 3

What Happens Now?

As we move forward knowing that the hard truth is needed in order to begin with a change, this is where you may be asking, *"What Happens Now?"* Well, the hardest part of change is accepting the problem and knowing that the problem needs a solution. Now that you are trying to evaluate what weaknesses you have that need work you need to know that not all days of this will be shiny and bright. To a disadvantage, with every decision of change comes temptation. Take a moment to reflect on what you have endured and how you felt during the moments that really hurt you. Using the hard truth of where you have been will have you reconsidering temptation. With growth comes challenges and unfortunately, they are just the parts of life that help us acquire knowledge and wisdom so that we can make better decisions for our future. God put you and me and even the ones you have betrayed us on this journey to create in us who *He* designed us to be for *His* purpose.

Everyone has their own destiny and with that comes different obstacles. We all have a breaking point and only so many of us have the interest in improving our lives, while others would rather remain in their comfort zone. Never lose yourself in the process of trying to gain someone else. Ignoring your needs and wants over someone else's will cause you heartbreak later on down the road. Setting some short-term goals will help you receive the most out of what life has to offer, as long as you have the drive to pursue them. These goals do not have to be accepted by anyone else and you should never feel you are unworthy of success just because your partner is insecure. You can actually pick up on jealousy and envy through conversation. Always strive to be great even if it means being great alone.

So, what happens now depends on YOU. Ask yourself what talents did God bless you with that you can use to reach some of the goals you desire? Remember, you hold the key to the door that God has put you in front of. "What Happens Now?" *Ask yourself the following questions to assist in your growth.*

Self–Evaluation Questions

1. Do I recognize the changes I need to make? If yes, what are they? If no, then start by making a list of your personality traits and what some common characteristics are that could be worked on.

   ____

   ____

2. What are some short-term goals I would like to accomplish for myself?

   ____

   ____

3. How can I learn to love myself the way I pour love into others?

   ____

   ____

Chapter 4

Peace & Healing

Now that you have accepted all the sections you will need to assist in your growth, here is the most amazing part. *Peace.*

Once you have come to terms with the fact that you have only hindered yourself from the best that you deserve, peace will come followed by your forgiving yourself. We all have been in a situation where it is easy to blame someone else for what they have done to us. However, taking responsibility for what you allow and what you engage in will help you work through any guilt, shame, or burdens that are weighing you down. Forgiving yourself is not saying what happened was okay but it is saying that you acknowledge that you participated in a situation when you knew better. Once you admit to yourself that you played a major role in hurting yourself by making poor choices and decisions, the faster the peace and healing form within you.

The most amazing feeling is how free you feel following any relationship that was not designed for you. We all have involved ourselves in some form of an unhealthy relationship and may have questioned ourselves afterward if it was something that we did wrong. If you know you bent over backward for someone and did all you could to make a relationship work and you still got used, abused, or let down, then you have to see that situation for what it is. To a disadvantage, this means that the relationship wasn't meant to be because we are not always aligned with people we think is good for us.

A good moment here and there does not mean that we will have a fulfilling life with that person. Some people can be loved unconditionally while for others you have to learn to love from a distance. Not everyone you encounter is going to make you happy and that is just a part of life. What is good to us is not always good for us. My last relationship started like a fairy tale and ended in the most abusive way I ever experienced in my life. I felt so free, happy, and amazing… I felt as though I won the Jackpot.

We have to want peace within our lives to get it and that includes eliminating anyone or anything that comes in the way of that. As for me, I knew better but I was a fighter, not a quitter. I didn't want my relationship to fail because people on the outside were making bets on how long it would last.

By thinking that my love language could heal the broken parts of someone else, I sacrificed my peace, my privacy, and my relationship with myself. As a result, I paid the price. Ignoring the red flags just because I wanted to see the goodness and potential in someone else cost me my money, my time, my investments, my family, my well-being, and how I perceived everything around me.

I want to inspire someone through this book to never tolerate this type of behavior or deal with anyone with toxic or narcissistic personality disorder. As stated, in Google, Narcissistic Personality Disorder is defined as a person who has an excessive need for admiration, disregard for others' feelings, an inability to handle any criticism, and a sense of entitlement. People with these traits also have countless insecurities. In most cases, whatever they accuse you of is only confessions of their own wrongdoing. If you feel you are in hell, then you may have encountered one. Just run. *In my next book, I will go into more detail about some personal experiences that changed my life.*

In addition, you create your own peace by loving yourself to the point where you know when you are settling for less than you deserve. In some cases, you may know someone who is in a relationship with someone who is constantly giving and not receiving what they give in return. A relationship will not succeed without reciprocity.

Google defines reciprocity as the practice of exchanging things with others for mutual benefit. So, if you find yourself sad, upset, angry, frustrated, and aggravated far more than you feel content and joyous, I'm sad to say that you are making yourself miserable in a situation that you will not grow in. *Is pleasing someone else worth you losing your peace?*

Along with peace, comes healing. The process of healing comes after you have forgiven yourself for participating in what you knew was not for you. Once you begin to heal you will begin to question what you have even seen in that person. The atmosphere in which you heal cannot be the same place that hurt you. At some point in the healing process, you will need to accept the fact that you may not get any type of closure from the person who hurt you, especially if you have been involved with a narcissist. They will never give you any type of closure because they use that as a way to return to you like nothing ever happened. As for you, staying no contact and far away from them as possible is your best option.

In the next chapter, I will point out some ways to notice signs and red flags that can show you if you are, in fact, a narcissist. Also, there are ways to disengage before they make you fall for them. Once you fall for them it is hard to walk away because, by this time, they have convinced you that they are this amazing person, when in fact, they are mimicking your behavior so you will fall quickly.

Along with healing, you will need to protect your peace by creating some strong boundaries. Boundaries are designed to show people what you will and will not tolerate. You are teaching someone how to treat you based on what you will and will not tolerate. Take the step of healing and beware of signs that do not sit right with your spirit. It is your priority to maintain your peace and take control over what you want in life and what you don't want. *Now, ask yourself the following questions.*

Self-Evaluation Questions

1. Have I forgiven myself?

   ____

   ____

2. Am I at peace in my life right now?

   ____

   ____

3. What is holding me back from healing?

   ____

   ____

4. Have I been involved with a narcissist or am I the narcissist?

   ____

   ____

5. What have others' actions shown me in my relationships?

   ____

   ____

24

Chapter 5

Red Flags

So, by now you should be admiring your freedom and your peace. As you continue to maintain your peace you will become stronger in what you deserve. The strength you gain will not only help you acknowledge personal faults, but it will encourage you to be firm about how you deserve to be treated. As you heal you are more susceptible to identifying the red flags that are associated with toxic and unhealthy relationships.

As for myself, I was able to identify some red flags in the beginning but being hardheaded made me learn the hard way. Red flags are signs of unhealthy, toxic, or manipulative behavior. I overlooked them and things would change just because the moment "felt right." Also, I was three months out of a divorce so the feeling of being amazing to someone felt like I had met the right person. I knew better because I knew I needed to heal from my marriage before I should have been with someone else.

Making yourself aware of character traits that highlight red flags can prevent some situations and eliminate the hurt that we tend to overlook if we are careful. The signs below can help identify if you are dealing with someone who is a narcissist or someone with toxic behavior.

1. ***Love-bombing*** is when the person is constantly giving you flattery, compliments, and affection. It can come in various forms, from giving gifts, sending long messages expressing how they feel, social media interactions, and passionate declarations of love.

2. ***Gaslighting*-** manipulating someone where they question their own sanity. For example, when you

have proof, they did something, and they still deny that it took place. Basically, lying and contradicting what you know is true.

3. ***People-pleasing-*** someone who bends over backwards to please others, even at their own expense. A false belief that someone will like you based on what you do for them, not because of who you are as a person.

4. ***Inconsistent behavior-*** unpredictable behavior, words not matching actions, standing you up on plans, and they don't make much of an effort.

5. ***Secretive/Sneaky-*** when they frequently lie to you or keep secrets.

6. ***Constantly referring to an ex-*** this shows that they have not fully moved on, and they may be using you as a rebound.

Please keep signs in mind that may detect red flags in your relationship. Learning how to love yourself more and giving yourself the love that you freely give to others will help you in future endeavors. The longer that you ignore the red flags the more toxic your relationship will become. Keeping your eyes open to these signals can save you the future incompatibility that will arise through lies, infidelity, and disrespect. You have control over what you tolerate. Don't forget that! Answer the following self-evaluation questions to enhance your growth.

Self-Evaluation Questions

1. What red flags have I overlooked?

    ____

    ____

2. What has my intuition been telling me about my current or previous relationship?

    ____

    ____

3. Now that I know the signs, have I seen 2 or more in my current or previous relationship?

    ____

    ____

4. Have I fallen for someone before realizing they were toxic?

    ____

    ____

Dazzling **SCARS**

30

Chapter 6

NEVER Overplay Your Role

If we are the ones who just so happen to get hurt during a relationship break-up, we always sit back and ask the question, "After as good as I have been to them, how could someone do me like that?" We ask that question over and over without asking, "Why couldn't I see the signs?" "Why did I tolerate that behavior knowing I deserved better?" I will be the one to tell you why we find ourselves tolerating what we don't deserve. We think the way we love is so deep and powerful and if we love hard our love can show them what true love should be like. Therefore, they will love us that way in return. WRONG!!

With this type of thinking we always fall short. Not everyone is designed with the same heart as you or me. Not everyone knows how to love unconditionally. Many people are cold and selfish with no emotion or remorse for how they treat others. With that being said, we have to realize that sometimes we can be "too much" for those that don't know how to love like us. As time moves forward it only reveals to us how we were better off leaving them where they were to begin with. I hate to be the one to break it to you all, but you cannot love the pain and unhealed versions out of someone, especially someone that runs from one person to the next without the dedication and discipline to heal. An unhealed person does not have any empathy and they do not care how they treat people. Sadly, they only care about what benefits them. So, NEVER overplay your role. Take the time to learn who may be attracted to you and for whatever reason. There is never a good enough reason to rush because you will rush in to rush out. Make sure you have had enough time to love yourself so that you know what you deserve. Loving "self" will save you many nights of hurt from engaging with toxic individuals.

As a woman myself, I understand that we like to do thoughtful things for our partners that show them they are loved and appreciated, but if you do too much without any reciprocity you may be attracting those individuals who use and abuse you. If someone really does care about you, they will care about how they make you feel. Just as you want to see them happy, that should be a mutual feeling between the both of you. We deserve a relationship where we can be ourselves and our partner loves every smile, every roll, the way you represent a rockstar when you wake up in the morning, etc.

You deserve to be complimented and never feel like you are competing with another person over your partner. With this being said, a real man will never put you in a situation that involves drama of any kind. A man who cares about you will move with care. He will build with you and not tear you down. He will encourage you and not belittle you. He may disagree with you, but he will not disrespect you. He will protect you and love you the way that God instructs. Never put yourself in a situation where you find yourself doing more for someone else than you would do for yourself. *Answer the following self-evaluation questions.*

Self-Evaluation Questions

1. Do I find myself rushing into relationships? If yes, why? What is the rush?

   ____

   ____

2. Looking at my current/past relationships, have I overplayed my role? If yes, do I consider myself a people-pleaser?

   ____

   ____

3. When getting to know someone, how do I keep myself from emotional attachment?

   ____

   ____

4. Why do I make excuses for someone's toxic behavior?

   ____

   ____

Chapter 7

YOU are the Prize.
ACT LIKE IT!!!

You know who you are. So, I am sure throughout this book you have asked yourself numerous times why you would even tolerate something when that is not who you are. When you recognize that you have tolerated things you normally wouldn't then you know you are more deserving of what you have been settling for. We all have done things in our lives that we aren't proud of, but that doesn't make us bad people. It is just a part of life. Without challenges and adversity, we would never grow. A bad person will usually possess disrespectful behavior, hurtful language, and actions, while disregarding your opinions and feelings, and never taking accountability for their actions.

On the contrary, a good person holds characteristics of honesty, integrity, kindness, and respect for others, is open to constructive criticism, and is willing to go the extra mile to make their partner feel good. When your partner's happiness is just as important as your own then your heart is in the right place. Deep down inside of you, you know who you are and what you stand for, so don't settle for less.

Strive for the absolute best that you deserve. Always remind yourself that YOU are the prize so ACT LIKE IT!!! *Answer the self-evaluation questions below.*

Self-Evaluation Questions

1. From this day forward, what changes can I make that will make me wiser in my future relationships?

   ____

   ____

2. How and what will I do to maintain my peace?

   ____

   ____

3. Now that I have read this book, I ask myself, "What is it that I stand for?"

   ____

   ____

Conclusion

I wrote this self-help book "Dazzling Scars" to inspire others and let them know we are not our scars. We are not the pain and grief we have endured. Through the hard truth, acceptance, forgiveness, healing, the scars of disappointment, guilt, and shame, have grown the strength and wisdom that shines from within our souls.

"Dazzling Scars" was written to show others how to evaluate themselves and how to apply those resolutions to their everyday relationships. With that being said, ladies and gentlemen, let your scars dazzle with the future blessings that you deserve.

42

About the Author

udrey Adams was born and raised in Cicero, which is a suburb outside the city of Chicago, Illinois. She currently resides in Valdosta, Georgia, near her immediate family.

Audrey is a compassionate, ambitious, and genuine woman who always looks for the goodness in others. However, to a disadvantage, she has experienced a few unhealthy/abusive relationships in the past, which has motivated her to help others recognize unhealthy patterns that can prevent failed relationships in the future.

To an advantage, by joining the YouTube channel created by Hario Ovadtop, which focuses on narcissistic relationships, Audrey gained knowledge through her personal experience with dating a narcissist. She has strived to be that voice that some may be ashamed to use. She desires to help many women and men across the globe find themselves again through self-evaluation strategies that can be applied to personal relationships.